The Skullys

MANIFESTO

EVERYONE DIES
NOT EVERYONE LIVES

FERNANDO ACEVEDO

To my family, who has given me the only thing
I have of true value in this world—the love that
shaped my life and the memories that I'll take
with me when I leave. Thank you.
I Love You.

Throughout my life I always heard a soft whisper in my ear saying "Live... Live... Live..."
It was death.

Dedication

To the dreamers, the artists, and the creators of this world who feel too much and think too deeply.

To those who keep hope alive by believing in something greater.
A higher power. A deeper meaning.

To those who believe this world is magic, that nothing is a coincidence, because everything happens for a reason.

To the ones who stare up at the night sky wondering if they're the only ones.

To the quiet souls whose voices get drowned out by the noise of the world,
whose thoughts run deeper than surface conversations ever allow.

To the lonely hearts who just need someone to say: You matter.
To the ones holding on by a thread, waiting for a reason not to let go.

To those who believe in kindness, even when it's mocked, and see it as virtue, not weakness.

To the ones who still open doors, speak gently, and give more than they take.

To those who believe that being meek is not weakness, but power under control.

To those who know that the nice guy doesn't always finish last, he just finishes with integrity.

And to the ones who have let their flames dim under the weight of others' expectations, drifting through days, feeling disconnected from their own dreams and desires, and say to themselves, there's got to be more to life than this.

May these words serve as the spark to reignite your fire and restore your passion to truly live again and be a light when the world feels dim.
A mirror when you feel invisible.
And a battle cry for your soul when it forgets how strong it really is.

This is for you.

You're not alone.

You are the reason this book exists.

Acknowledgments

This book began as a whisper.
A quiet ache in my heart.
A burning question I couldn't shake:
This is it? Get a job, pay bills, check off items
from a list, travel when I'm old then wait to die?
There's got to be more to life than this, right?

It became an endless search for purpose and
meaning.

I'm still searching...

To God: Thank You for the mystery of Faith.
Thank You for the moments when I broke, and
the strength You gave me to build something
from the rubble, and for the opportunity to
experience this beautiful thing called life.

To the family I was born into:
My mother and father who struggled and
sacrificed so much in their lives to raise their
children as best they could. Thank you!
My two brothers, the only thing I have of true
value in my life are the moments I shared with
you growing up. Thank you for never giving up
on me!

To my chosen family and friends:
Thank you for never letting me hit rock bottom
and offering a helping hand when I needed to get
up. A bit of tough love mixed with unconditional
love gave me the strength to always keep
moving forward. Thank you for letting me be

unfinished, uncertain, and deeply human.
Thank you for giving me space to grow and the
grace to come back better.

To everyone who ever believed in me, even when
I didn't believe in myself, thank you.
Your love, your presence, your patience gave me
the strength to keep writing when all I wanted to
do was disappear.

To the people who challenged me, hurt me, broke
me open, thank you too. You were part of this
story. You helped shape the voice behind these
words.

To every dreamer, poet, and philosopher whose
words lit a match in the dark, your wisdom flows
through these pages.

To the ones who've struggled, who've searched,
who've suffered quietly. You were the ones I had
in mind every time I sat down to write.
I hope these words met you where you are.

And finally, to the reader:
If this book reached you, helps you, heals you in
some way, then it did what it was meant to do.

Thank you for being part of this.

— Fernando Acevedo

"Shyness is nice,
and shyness can stop you
from doing all the things in life
that you'd like to"
— Morrissey

Table of Contents

Introduction

Everyone Dies, Not Everyone Lives.

People who wake up in the morning are alive.
But only a few are actually living.

We get up. Check our phones. Drown in noise.
Go to jobs we hate. Chase approval we don't need.
Numb the ache with caffeine, scrolling, alcohol, porn, distraction.

Then one day, we look up and wonder where the hell our life went. 30 years went by in the blink of an eye.

The average human expectancy is **just 77 years**. That's it.
You'll spend about **26 of those years sleeping**.
Between **13 -15 years working**.
And nearly **12 full years just looking at a screen**.

You weren't born to survive a job.
You weren't born to be a working consumer.
You weren't put here to pay bills, and coast into a quiet death.

You were made to ignite. To feel deeply. To risk, love, scream, fail, rise, and do something that matters, before the lights go out.

But most people die before they're dead.

They quit on their dreams. They bury their truth.
They trade authenticity for acceptance and they call it "being realistic."

This is not a book for the realistic.
The Skullys Manifesto is a declaration of war against the half-lived life. It's a rebellion against the numbness.
The mediocrity.

The safety that suffocates us, and yet we spend most of our lives working towards.

These words are a pulse-check.
A mirror.
A middle finger.
A battle cry for those who still want more from themselves, from life, from the fire in their chest.

We're here to talk about **what it means to be human**.
To live with purpose. To stand for something. To remember that this life short, messy, beautiful, brutal and it is the only one we get.

You can't live forever. But you can live fully.
And that starts now.

WELCOME TO

MANIFESTO

Prologue

We all feel it.

That low hum just beneath the surface.
The quiet panic that comes when we're alone.
The ache we try to drown in work, in noise, in comfort.
It's the awareness, however faint, that time is slipping through our fingers.

And still, we wait.

We wait for the right time. The right mood. The right circumstances.
We wait to feel ready, bold, perfect.
We wait so long, we forget what we were waiting for.

But death doesn't wait.
It doesn't care if your dreams are unfinished or if your heart still has more to say.

It comes for everyone, the loud, the quiet, the daring, the dull.

And when it does, you realize that you never really lived.

They followed the rules.
Played it safe.
Kept their heads down.
Fit in.

They survived.
But they never truly tasted life.
Never lit the fire.
Never danced in the chaos.
Never spoke their truth, chased their calling, or loved with reckless courage.

This book isn't about fear.
It's about *impermanence* and It's about *remembrance*.

That life is wild, short, and unpredictable.
That you have no obligation to become who the world expects.

That the ones who live fully are rarely the ones who had it easy, they're the ones who chose to feel it all.

This manifesto is for the ones who are done sleepwalking.
The ones who crave more than just existence.
The ones who know, deep down, that this is it.
The clock is ticking.

But it hasn't stopped.
And as long as you're still breathing,

there's still time to begin.

Chapter 1
The Clock Is Ticking

You think you have time. You don't.

"You could leave life right now. Let that determine what you do and say and think."
— Marcus Aurelius

We live like we're immortal.
We scroll past the seconds.
We postpone our dreams.
We make plans for "someday" like it's promised, like it's ours.

But time doesn't care what you meant to do or what your
intentions were. It slips quietly. Softly. Without warning.
You don't hear it. You don't feel it.
And by the time you notice, it's already gone.

The average human lifespan is just **4,000 weeks**.
By the time you're 30, nearly half of those are already spent.
Let that sink in.

A man once told his son, "I'll spend more time with you
when I retire."
He never made it to retirement.

A woman waited until her kids were grown to write her book.
They left home. The book was never written.

Another saved money for years to travel the world, and died
just before his first flight.

Things like this happen every single day and yet we take it so
lightly because it doesn't affect us directly. Until it does.

We tell ourselves there will be time later.
But later is a liar.
It's the softest, deadliest form of self-betrayal.
We tell ourselves that we'll do it someday but someday
doesn't exist. We're all on borrowed time so don't waste
it on someday

"You may delay, but time will not."
— Benjamin Franklin

In the Qur'an:
"By time, surely man is in loss..."
— Surah Al-Asr 103:1—2

In the Torah:
"Teach us to number our days, that we may gain a heart of wisdom."
— Psalm 90:12

The Stoics carved it into every morning:
Memento Mori — Remember: you will die.
This is not meant to scare you.
It's meant to free you.

Stop waiting for clarity.
Stop waiting to feel ready.
Stop putting off the life that's already slipping past you.
You don't need more time.
You need more urgency.

This moment is all you have.
Burn it.
Love it.
Live like your soul is on fire, because it is.

The clock is ticking.
But you're still here.
And that means you still have a chance to live like it matters.

Borrowed Time
Time is not yours.
It is borrowed breath,
fading light,
a sandglass tipping while you scroll.
Don't waste it on "someday."
Use it while it's still yours to spend.

"The problem is, you think you have time."
—Jack Kornfield

Take a moment to think about what you have read.
Let it sink in a bit. Then let the following questions be a
guide to where you are, and where you want to be.
Take a moment and really think about them.

Reflections:

• What am I putting off because I believe there's still "time"?

• If I had one year left, what would I stop doing?

• What would I start today?

Chapter 2
Surviving Isn't Living

**There's a difference between not being dead
and being truly alive.**

*"To live is the rarest thing in the world.
Most people exist, that is all."*
— Oscar Wilde

Some people die young.
Others live to ninety.
But the real tragedy is how many die inside...
and no one notices for decades.
They're not six feet under, they're just six layers deep in
denial, routine, and quiet resignation.

You can be alive
and still be starving for oxygen.
You can breathe
and still feel like you're drowning.

Survival is basic.
It's instinct.
Wake up. Eat. Work. Repeat.
It's not life—it's maintenance.

Living, really living, is something else entirely.
It's risk. It's love. It's loss. It's meaning.
It's fire in the lungs, not just air.
It's presence, not just persistence.

Some people don't resist death.
They resist life.
Because life hurts.
Because life demands.
Because living requires that you feel it all, not just the good
stuff. Life requires you to suffer so that you may know joy.

*"Man is not made for defeat. A man can
be destroyed but not defeated."*
— Ernest Hemingway

There are people who have nothing, and still greet the day dancing.
There are people with everything, and yet they are ghosts in their own homes.

Survival depends on biology.
Living depends on intention.

What if you started making decisions, not based on fear, but on the life you actually want?

You weren't born just to endure.
You were born to shine.
To feel deeply.
To live fully.
To matter.

"We suffer more in imagination than in reality."
— Seneca

"Don't confuse having a pulse with being alive."
— The Skullys

The Half-Life
I was breathing,
but I wasn't alive.
I was eating,
but I wasn't fed.
I was safe, and dying slowly in the cage of my comfort.
Until I remembered that the heart is a wild thing,
and I had kept it muzzled for too long.

"A ship in harbor is safe,
but that's not what ships are for."
—John A. Shedd

Take a moment to think about what you have read.
Let it sink in a bit. Then let the following questions be a
guide to where you are, and where you want to be.
Take a moment and really think about them.

Reflections:
• Am I living by design or just by default?

• What's one part of my life I'm just "surviving" through?

• If fear wasn't a factor, what would I pursue?

Chapter 3
Burn the Script

The life you were told to live isn't the one you came here for.

"You must be willing to let go of the life you planned so as to have the life that is waiting for you."
— Joseph Campbell

You were handed a script the day you were born.
It was written by parents, teachers, culture, tradition.
It told you who you were supposed to be.
What success looked like.
Who to love.
How to dress.
What to chase.
What to fear.
What not to question.
You memorized the lines.
You played the part.
And maybe it worked...
until one day, it didn't.

You woke up.
Not fully. Not all at once.
Just enough to realize:
this life doesn't fit.

The suit fits,
but it's not yours.
The lines are perfect,
but they're not true.

"Until you make the unconscious conscious,
it will direct your life and you will call it fate."
— Carl Jung

Burning the script doesn't mean you're ungrateful.
It means you're finally honest.
Honest enough to ask:
Who am I when I'm not performing?
What do I want when no one is watching?
What would I create if I wasn't afraid of being wrong?

You're not broken.
You're just awakening.
And awakening is brutal.
It requires grief, for the life you thought you'd live,
and courage, for the one you're now choosing.
There's a version of you
on the other side of obedience.
That version won't settle.
Won't fake it.
Won't dim.

That version is waiting for you!

Your life isn't a performance.
Rip up the script.
Say your own lines.
Walk off the stage.
And write a story that makes your soul feel alive.

"If you don't build your own dream,
someone will hire you to build theirs."
— Tony Gaskins

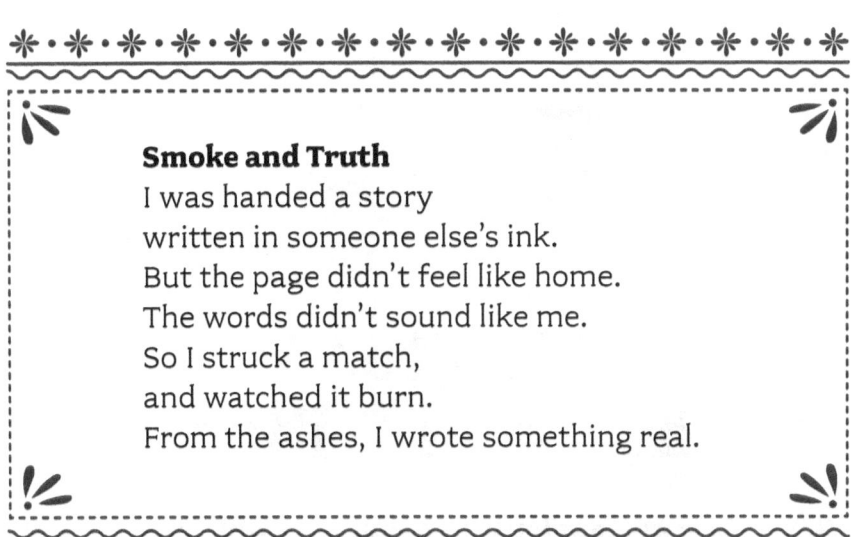

Smoke and Truth
I was handed a story
written in someone else's ink.
But the page didn't feel like home.
The words didn't sound like me.
So I struck a match,
and watched it burn.
From the ashes, I wrote something real.

*"You are under no obligation to be the same
person you were five minutes ago."*
— Alan Watts

*"Your time is limited, so don't waste
it living someone else's life."*
— Steve Jobs

Take a moment to think about what you have read.
Let it sink in a bit. Then let the following questions be a
guide to where you are, and where you want to be.
Take a moment and really think about them.

Reflections:
• What parts of my life are running on autopilot?

• Whose voice am I trying to please at the expense of my own?

• What's one "rule" I'm ready to break in order to be more free?

Chapter 4
The Art of Stillness

The world is loud. But your soul whispers.

*"All of humanity's problems stem from man's
inability to sit quietly in a room alone."*
— Blaise Pascal

We glorify the hustle culture.
We confuse being busy with being productive.
We wear stress like a badge.
We mistake movement for progress, and noise for meaning.

But the truth is, some of the loudest lives are the most hollow.

There is power in **stillness** but it is a lost art.
And in a world addicted to motion, stillness is rebellion.

*"If you cannot find peace within yourself,
you will never find it anywhere else."*
— Marvin Gaye

We fill our days so we don't have to feel.
We scroll past the ache.
We binge distraction like it's medicine.
But there's a deeper pain we avoid:
the pain of meeting ourselves.

The Stoics practiced it.
The monks devoted lifetimes to it.
Jesus escaped to the wilderness.
Muhammad climbed a mountain.
Buddha sat under a tree.

Stillness isn't the absence of life, it's the return to it.
Stillness doesn't mean doing nothing.
It means becoming aware.

Aware of what you're running from.
Aware of what matters.
Aware that you are alive, here, now and this moment is enough.

The Tao Te Ching says:
"To the mind that is still, the whole universe surrenders."

And Rainer Maria Rilke whispers:
"Have patience with everything unresolved... live the questions now."

Stillness is not weakness.
It is radical presence.
It is where clarity is born.
It is where the noise falls away and the truth rises.

You don't need to chase your life.
You just need to return to it.

"Be still and know that I am God."
— Psalm 46:10

The Whisper

When was the last time you heard your own breath?
Not in the rush between emails or traffic lights, but in
that soft, ancient silence where your soul lives?

Sit with it. It hurts at first—because silence doesn't lie.
But if you're brave, it will tell you who you are.

"Silence is the sleep that nourishes wisdom."
— Francis Bacon

*"Within you, there is a stillness and a sanctuary to
which you can retreat at any time."*
— Hermann Hesse

Take a moment to think about what you have read.
Let it sink in a bit. Then let the following questions be a
guide to where you are, and where you want to be.
Take a moment and really think about them.

Reflections:

• When was the last time I was still with no agenda, no phone,
no goal, just breath?

• What part of me am I avoiding in the silence?

Chapter 5
Everyone Dies,
Not Everyone Lives

You came here to stand out. Not to blend in.

"It is not length of life, but depth of life."
— Ralph Waldo Emerson

Everyone dies.
You will. I will.
Every single person you love will become dust and memory.
But death isn't the tragedy.
The tragedy is this:

Most people never really live.

They coast and drift through life.
They tolerate.
They follow the script.
They silence their instincts.
They swallow their pain and call it "being strong."

But inside... inside they're screaming.
Inside, they know:
There's more than this.
More than bills.
More than fear.
More than fitting in.

Living isn't surviving.
Living is waking up.
Burning bright. Risking love.
Saying what you mean.
Doing what calls you, even if no one claps.

*"There is no greater agony than bearing
an untold story inside you."*
— Maya Angelou

Marcus Aurelius wrote:
"It is not death that a man should fear, but never beginning to live."

And in the Qur'an:
"Every soul shall taste death." (Surah Al-Imran 3:185)

But it says nothing about every soul truly living.
Because **life is a choice.**

And most people say no without realizing it.
They say no to dreams.
No to love.
No to healing.
No to starting over.
They call it "being realistic."
But what it is... is *fear in disguise*.
There is a you inside you—braver, louder, freer.

A version **unafraid of living fully**.

That version is waiting.
And maybe it's time to stop dying in slow motion and start living on purpose.

"Cowards die many times before their deaths."
— William Shakespeare

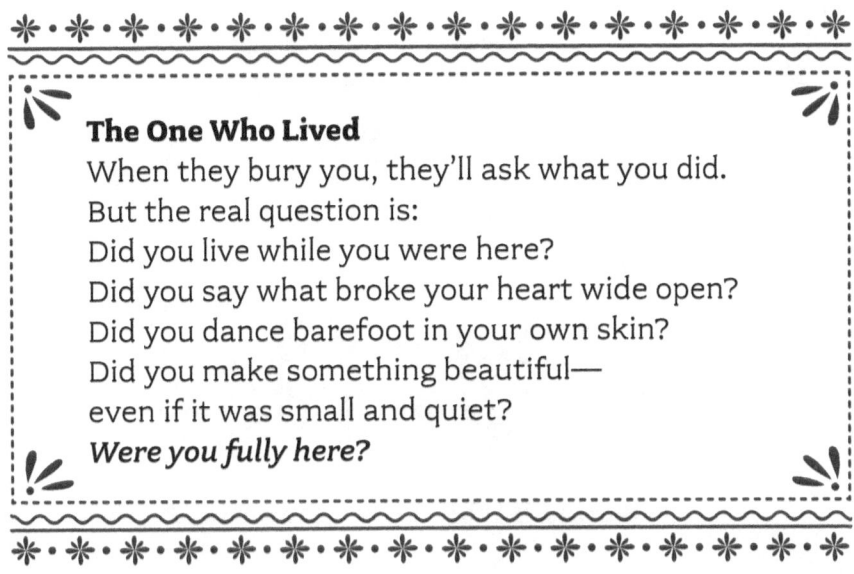

The One Who Lived

When they bury you, they'll ask what you did.
But the real question is:
Did you live while you were here?
Did you say what broke your heart wide open?
Did you dance barefoot in your own skin?
Did you make something beautiful—
even if it was small and quiet?
Were you fully here?

*"Don't ask what the world needs. Ask what
makes you come alive, and go do it."*
— Howard Thurman

Take a moment to think about what you have read.
Let it sink in a bit. Then let the following questions be a
guide to where you are, and where you want to be.
Take a moment and really think about them.

Reflections:

• What would I do differently if I truly believed I was running
out of time?

• What does "really living" look like for me, not anyone else?

Chapter 6
The Sacred Pain

The wound is where the light enters.

"To live is to suffer, to survive is to find meaning in the suffering."
— Friedrich Nietzsche

Pain is not a punishment.
It is a portal.
It cracks open the parts of you that were sealed too tight.
It strips away illusion, control, pride.
It reminds you that you are **fragile. Human. Alive.**

And that's not a curse, it's a sacred invitation.

We've been trained to run from pain.
To numb it, medicate it, mask it.
But pain isn't the enemy.

Pain is the uninvited teacher
that shows up when the soul is ready to grow.

The Stoics knew this well.
*"If you are distressed by anything external, the pain is not
due to the thing itself, but to your estimate of it."*
— Marcus Aurelius

In other words: Pain breaks you.
Then it asks: **will you rebuild stronger, or stay shattered?**

"Out of suffering have emerged the strongest souls."
— Khalil Gibran

In the **Buddhist tradition**, pain is part of the First Noble Truth:

Life is *suffering*.
But not meaningless suffering.
Transformative suffering.

In Christianity
"Even though I walk through the valley of the shadow of death, I will fear no evil."
— Psalm 23:4

Even in the darkest of times. Those who have faith will not feel alone or afraid in the face of adversity because of God's presence, guidance and protection.

Grief. Betrayal. Loneliness. Failure.
These are not signs that something has gone wrong.
These are the waters where the soul drowns—and then learns to breathe.

Remember that diamonds are made under immense pressure and can not be polished without friction, as a man can not be made better without trials.

Tough times or challenges can lead to personal growth and the development of valuable qualities. The pressure we experience in life can be a catalyst for transformation and strength.

"Sometimes when you're in a dark place you think you've been buried, but you've actually been planted"
— Christine Caine

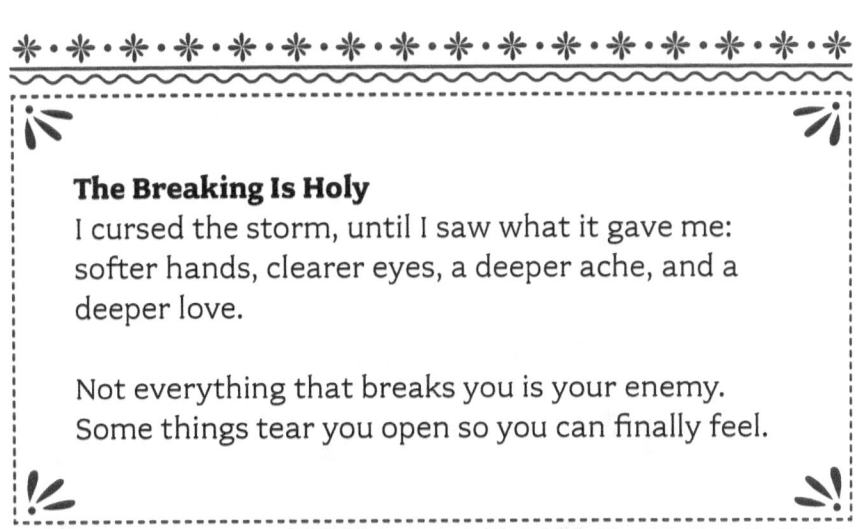

The Breaking Is Holy
I cursed the storm, until I saw what it gave me:
softer hands, clearer eyes, a deeper ache, and a
deeper love.

Not everything that breaks you is your enemy.
Some things tear you open so you can finally feel.

"Do not be afraid of pain.
Be afraid of a life so guarded that nothing can
touch you, not even joy."
— The Skullys

Take a moment to think about what you have read.
Let it sink in a bit. Then let the following questions be a
guide to where you are, and where you want to be.
Take a moment and really think about them.

Reflections:
• What has my pain taught me that joy never could?

• Am I avoiding something sacred by trying to stay comfortable?

Chapter 7
The Wild Ones

They weren't made to follow. They were made to feel everything and burn bright.

"The reasonable man adapts himself to the world... the unreasonable one persists in trying to adapt the world to himself. Therefore, all progress depends on the unreasonable man."
— George Bernard Shaw

They don't fit in.
They never did.
Not in the classroom. Not in the boardroom.
Not in the boxes society keeps trying to shove them into.
The Wild Ones don't obey the script.
They write their own.
They laugh too loud, cry too much, dream too big.
They risk being misunderstood, because being fake would be worse.

These are your people.

And if you're reading this chapter with your pulse rising...
you're probably one of them.

They are the artists.
The wanderers.
The ones who say the quiet thing out loud.
The ones who leave comfort behind to follow something invisible.
Not because it's easy, but because it's true.

"Do not conform to the pattern of this world, but be transformed by the renewing of your mind."
— Romans 12:2

"Tell me, what is it you plan to do with your one wild and precious life?"
— Mary Oliver

The Wild Ones were never here to settle.
They are here to stir. To wake. To disrupt.
To remind the world that conformity is not the price of peace, it is the death of the soul.

They are not fearless.
They feel everything, deeper than most.
That's why they need solitude.
And that's why they crave realness like oxygen.

The Stoics would admire their discipline.
The mystics would recognize their longing.
The prophets would say they're chosen.
Because being wild isn't about chaos.
It's about authenticity.
It's about living in alignment with the fire in your chest,
even when it makes people uncomfortable.

"I do not believe that the same God who endowed us with sense, reason, and intellect intended us to forgo their use."
— Galileo Galilei

If you feel like you don't belong, it's because you were never meant to fit, you were meant to lead.
Not with a title, but with your truth.
So stay wild, stay awake, let your weird be sacred, and your fire stay lit.

We need you.

The Ones Who Run with Wolves
They said,
"You're too much."
And I said,
"That's the point."
My fire doesn't need your permission.
My truth doesn't need your applause.
I was not made to be small.
I was made to howl.

"When we are no longer able to change a situation,
we are challenged to change ourselves."
— Viktor Frankl

"The most courageous act is still to think for
yourself. Aloud."
— Coco Chanel

Take a moment to think about what you have read.
Let it sink in a bit. Then let the following questions be a
guide to where you are, and where you want to be.
Take a moment and really think about them.

Reflections:

• Where in my life am I playing small to be accepted?

• What part of me feels "too much," and what if that part is
actually sacred?

Chapter 8
Fireproof

**They threw you into the fire.
They didn't know you were the flame.**

*"Do not pray for an easy life, pray for the
strength to endure a difficult one."*
— Bruce Lee

Some things break.
Some things bend.
But the sacred part of you?
The part forged in storms and sharpened in silence?
That part is **fireproof**.

You've been through enough by now to know:
Resilience isn't loud.
It doesn't flex.
It doesn't seek attention.

It just **endures**.

You didn't ask for the fire.
But it came.
In the form of heartbreak, betrayal, loss, failure.
And you thought it would destroy you.
It didn't.

It burned away what you didn't need.
What remained was forged—stronger than steel,
softer than truth.

"Hard times create strong men.
Strong men create good times.
Good times create weak men.
And weak men create hard times."
— G. Michael Hopf

It's a cycle.
And those who survive it?
They carry the medicine.
The wisdom.
The scars that shine in the dark.

The Stoics didn't preach avoidance.
They preached **acceptance and mastery.**

"You have power over your mind, not outside events.
Realize this, and you will find strength."
— Marcus Aurelius

Buddhism calls it *non-attachment*.
Christianity calls it *faith*.
Islam calls it *sabr*—patience in hardship.
Judaism calls it *emunah*—a deep trust that even what we
don't understand is sacred.

No matter the path, the message is the same:
You are more than what you've lost.
You are what the fire could not touch.

"Though I walk through the fire,
I will not be burned."
— Isaiah 43:2

"What you seek is seeking you."
— Rumi

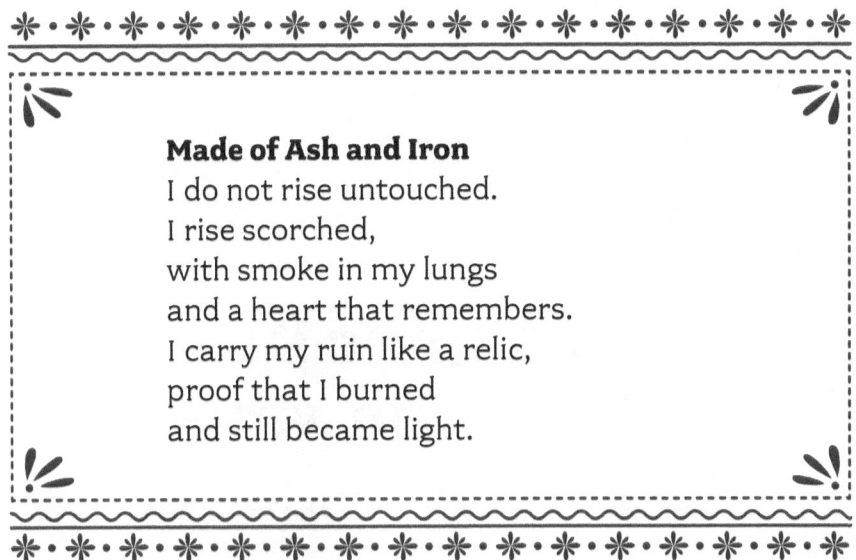

Made of Ash and Iron
I do not rise untouched.
I rise scorched,
with smoke in my lungs
and a heart that remembers.
I carry my ruin like a relic,
proof that I burned
and still became light.

"The fire didn't kill you. It crowned you."
— The Skullys

Take a moment to think about what you have read.
Let it sink in a bit. Then let the following questions be a
guide to where you are, and where you want to be.
Take a moment and really think about them.

Reflections:

• What has life burned away that I didn't actually need?

• What part of me remains unchanged, untouchable, no
matter what I go through?

• In what ways have I grown stronger, not in spite of the
pain, but because of it?

Chapter 9
The Hollowing

Emptiness isn't the end. It's the beginning.

*"Be empty of worrying.
Think of who created thought.
Why do you stay in prison when the
door is so wide open?"*
— Rumi

There is a silence that comes
after the chaos,
after the loss,
after the breaking.

Not the peace-kind of silence.
The empty kind.
The **hollow**.

It feels like nothing.
But it's not.
It's the space in which something new can finally take root.

The *Hollowing* happens when we lose what we thought we
couldn't live without.
A dream. A person. A version of ourselves.
And what's left behind is just... space.
It's terrifying.
But what if this emptiness is sacred?
What if it's the womb of becoming?

"When I let go of what I am, I become what I might be."
— Lao Tzu

"Blessed are the poor in spirit, for theirs
is the kingdom of heaven."
— Matthew 5:3

In the spiritual traditions, emptiness is not a problem.
It is the necessary stillness before creation.

The Buddhists call it **Śūnyatā**—a state beyond ego, beyond self, where true wisdom is born.
Mystics call it the dark night of the soul.
The desert.
The in-between.

But always—always—the hollowing is followed by the filling.

"The wound is where the light enters you."
— Rumi

"He who knows others is wise.
He who knows himself is enlightened."
— Lao Tzu

"The quieter you become, the more you can hear."
— Ram Dass

We fear emptiness.
But it's in emptiness that the Divine often speaks.
Not in the noise of *achievement*.
Not in the chaos of *desire*.
But in the sacred hush of *surrender*.

Sometimes life doesn't need to add more to you.
It needs to **carve you out** so you can hold more light.

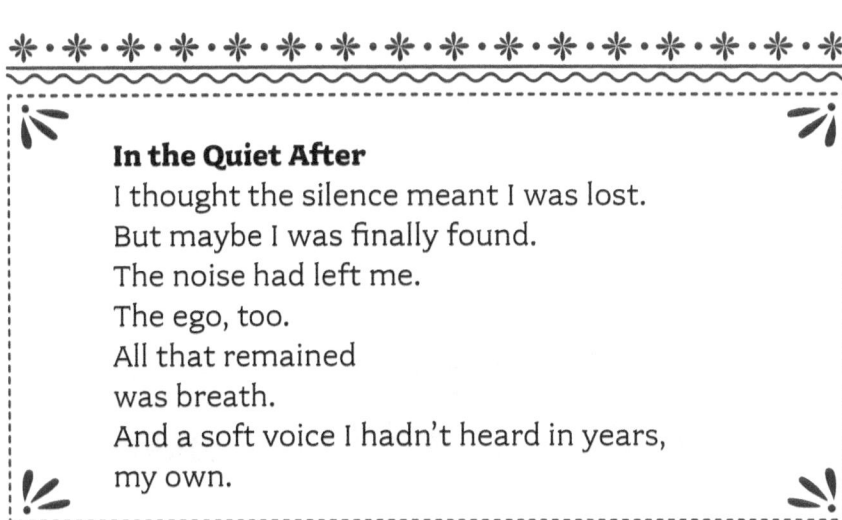

In the Quiet After
I thought the silence meant I was lost.
But maybe I was finally found.
The noise had left me.
The ego, too.
All that remained
was breath.
And a soft voice I hadn't heard in years,
my own.

*"The hollowing is not the end of you. It's the clearing
where your truest self is finally allowed to grow."*
— The Skullys

*"Only those who risk going too far can possibly find out
how far one can go."*
— T.S. Eliot

Take a moment to think about what you have read.
Let it sink in a bit. Then let the following questions be a
guide to where you are, and where you want to be.
Take a moment and really think about them.

Reflections:
• What have I lost that made space for something more
authentic?

• Where in my life do I feel hollow? What might that space
be *preparing* me for?

• Can I sit with emptiness without rushing to fill it?

Chapter 10
The Price of Freedom

**Money is never just money.
It's power. It's pressure. It's possibility.**

*"Wealth consists not in having great possessions,
but in having few wants."*
— Epictetus

Money touches every corner of human experience, and yet it's often cloaked in shame, illusion, or silence.

Money changes everything.
Where you live.
What you eat.
What kind of healthcare you get.
How much time you have for your own dreams.
Even how people treat you in a room.
To pretend otherwise is a lie.

There are two kinds of people:
those who are *free* to chase their passion,
and those who must survive.

If you've ever worked a job you hated just to keep the lights on, if you've ever watched your art die under the weight of bills and responsibilities, you know this truth intimately:

Money isn't evil. It's oxygen.
But it's also not the point.

Those born into privilege often romanticize struggle.
They wear poverty like an aesthetic.
But real lack is brutal.

It doesn't build character, it breaks backs.
There's no glory in choosing between rent and groceries.
No magic in being told to "just follow your passion"
when survival is the only thing on your to-do list.

And yet, those who have known lack often possess
something sacred: **Grit. Humility. Depth. Perspective. Fire.**

The struggle can strip you.
But it can also shape you into someone unstoppable.

*"It is not the man who has too little,
but the man who craves more, that is poor."*
— Seneca

Here's the paradox:
Money can buy you time, options, therapy, peace of mind.
But if you make it your god, it will devour your soul.

Work for money, and you may survive.
Work for meaning, and you may come alive.
Find a way to do both, and you win the game.

Some of the wealthiest people on earth are poor in soul.
And some of the poorest carry a richness that no account
balance can touch.

We are not here to worship money.
We are here to master it, to earn it honestly, spend it
wisely, give it freely, and never confuse it with who we are.

*"Too many people spend money they haven't earned
to buy things they don't want
to impress people they don't like."*
— Will Rogers

*"For what shall it profit a man, if he shall gain the
whole world, and lose his own soul?"*
— Mark 8:36

Bread and Fire
They told me to chase my dreams, but I had mouths
to feed. They said to "manifest abundance,"
while I was counting quarters.
It's hard to be grateful when you're living in debt and
your stomach is empty, I know.
But still—I never stopped writing, never stopped
building, because being broke exists only in the mind.
Even the broke can be rich in something deeper.

"Success is having to worry about every damn
thing in the world, except money."
—Johnny Cash

"Get the money. But never let it cost you your soul."
— The Skullys

Take a moment to think about what you have read.
Let it sink in a bit. Then let the following questions be a
guide to where you are, and where you want to be.
Take a moment and really think about them.

Reflections:
• Is my relationship with money based on fear, greed, guilt,
or freedom?

• What would I create if money weren't the issue?

• Am I surviving... or am I living?

Chapter 11
The Ones Who Stay Awake

Stay awake. Even when the world begs you to forget.

*"It is no measure of health to be well
adjusted to a profoundly sick society."*
—Jiddu Krishnamurti

Most people are asleep. Not asleep in bed— asleep in spirit.
The real epidemic isn't fatigue. It's spiritual sedation.

They rise, clock in, chase noise, silence their longing, scroll
endlessly, numb the ache, buy things they don't need, chase
goals they never chose, and call it "normal."
But normal is a lie.
Sleep is safe.
And awareness?
It's a rebellion.

To stay awake is to feel the **ache of being alive**.
To see suffering and not look away.
To question everything that doesn't make sense.
To live by **truth**, not trends.
You won't be applauded for staying awake.
You'll be misunderstood.

"Awakening is not changing who you are,
but discarding who you are not."
— *Deepak Chopra*

Too intense. Too sensitive. Too deep.
Because a world addicted to sedation
hates the ones who remember how to feel.

You'll meet others along the way.
Flickering candles in the dark.
People who ask the hard questions.
Who break instead of fake.

Who'd rather walk alone than belong to a lie.
Find them.
Keep them.
They are your tribe.

*"The awakened man is a warrior who faces
reality as it is, not as he wishes it to be."*
— Stoic teaching

"The mass of men lead lives of quiet desperation."
— Henry David Thoreau

Religious sages warned us:
"Watch and pray so that you will not fall asleep."
— Jesus, Matthew 26:41

"Be mindful, be vigilant."
— Buddha

*"He who remembers God standing, sitting, and lying on
their sides..."*
— Quran 3:191

Awareness isn't just mental.
It's sacred.
It's how you resist the slow death of routine.

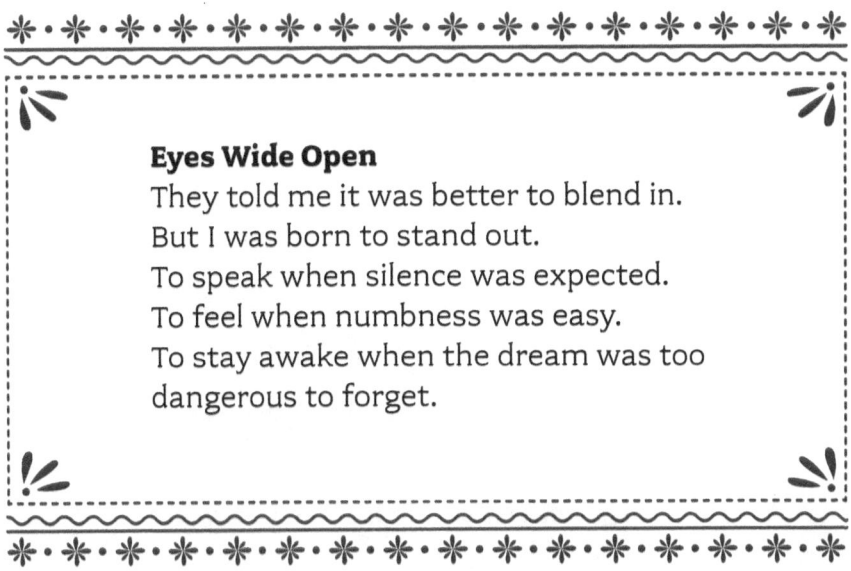

Eyes Wide Open
They told me it was better to blend in.
But I was born to stand out.
To speak when silence was expected.
To feel when numbness was easy.
To stay awake when the dream was too
dangerous to forget.

*"You either walk inside your story and own it, or
you stand outside and hustle for your worthiness."*
— Brené Brown

*"Stay awake. It will cost you comfort,
but it will buy you your life."*
— The Skullys

Take a moment to think about what you have read.
Let it sink in a bit. Then let the following questions be a
guide to where you are, and where you want to be.
Take a moment and really think about them.

Reflections:
• In what areas of my life am I sleepwalking?

• What truths am I afraid to face because they would
require change?

• What would it look like to live with eyes fully open?

Chapter 12
What Remains

You will be gone. But something of you will stay.

"Carve your name on hearts, not tombstones.
A legacy is etched into the minds of others
and the stories they share about you."
— Shannon L. Alder

Legacy: not in the shallow sense of wealth or fame, but in the echoes we leave behind. The imprints. The energy. The love. The scars. The truths. What remains of us when our body no longer does.

One day, your name will be spoken for the last time.
No one wants to think about it, but it's true:

You will die. And the world will keep spinning.

But while you're here, you're leaving fingerprints, on people, on places, on the very air.

The question is not **if** you'll leave a legacy.
It's **what kind**.

You don't need money.
You don't need children.
You don't need to be famous.
You just need to live like your life matters—**because it does**.

"The greatest use of a life is to spend it for
something that outlasts it."
— William James

"Do not seek to be remembered.
Seek to be unforgettable."
— The Skullys

Legacy isn't a monument.

It's *how you made someone feel* when they were breaking.
It's the *truth you spoke* when it was easier to stay silent.
It's the ripple of *courage you gave someone* too afraid to stand.

Your real legacy might never have your name on it.

But it will live.

Think of the people who shaped you.
Some are gone.
But something of them lives in you.
You are their living proof.
Their walking echo.

And now, you carry that same power.

*"A man's worth is not in what he owns, but in
what he leaves behind in others."*
— The Skullys

*"Try to live so that when you die, even the
undertaker will be sorry."*
— Mark Twain

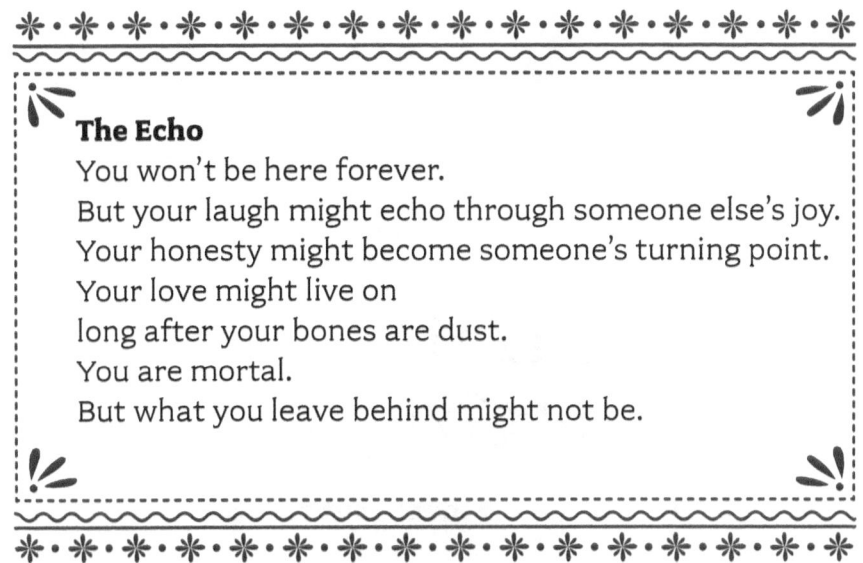

The Echo
You won't be here forever.
But your laugh might echo through someone else's joy.
Your honesty might become someone's turning point.
Your love might live on
long after your bones are dust.
You are mortal.
But what you leave behind might not be.

*"The meaning of life is to plant trees under whose
shade you do not expect to sit."*
— Nelson Henderson

You will die. But parts of you will live in others.
Live like that matters.
— The Skullys

Take a moment to think about what you have read.
Let it sink in a bit. Then let the following questions be a
guide to where you are, and where you want to be.
Take a moment and really think about them.

Reflections:

• If I disappeared today, what would people remember about me?

• Am I living in a way that echoes love, truth, and purpose?

• What am I planting that will grow after I'm gone?

Chapter 13
Forgiveness

Let go, not for them—but for you.

*"Holding onto anger is like drinking poison
and expecting the other person to die."*
— Buddha

Forgiveness is not a clean word.
It's not soft. It's not always noble.
Sometimes it's survival.

We talk about it like it's simple.
Say things like "forgive and forget" as if it's a light switch.
But real forgiveness is war.
And the battlefield is inside you.

There are people who hurt you.
Some knew. Some didn't.
Some said sorry. Most didn't.

They betrayed you, abandoned you, broke you in ways
they'll never understand.

But here's the truth:
You're the one still carrying it.
You're the one bleeding.
You're the one re-playing what happened like a film stuck
on repeat.

And the longer you carry it,
the heavier it becomes.
Forgiveness isn't forgetting.
It's not pretending.
It's not excusing.
It's releasing.
It's choosing to be free.
Not because they earned it.
But because you're tired of dragging the weight.

"To forgive is to set a prisoner free and
discover the prisoner was you."
— Lewis B. Smedes

Sometimes the person you need to forgive is you.
For the mistake.
For the failure.
For being human.
We're all doing the best we can with the pain we inherited.

Religions call it sacred:
"Forgive us our trespasses, as we forgive those who trespass against us."
— Christianity

"He who forgives and makes peace, his reward is due from Allah."
— Quran 42:40

"Hatred does not cease by hatred, but only by love."
— Buddha, Dhammapada

"The weak can never forgive.
Forgiveness is the attribute of the strong."
— Mahatma Gandhi

Forgiveness is divine not because it makes you holy,
but because it frees you from hell.

You don't have to forget.
You don't have to heal overnight.
But you do have to choose:
Do you want to stay in the prison,
or walk out the open door?

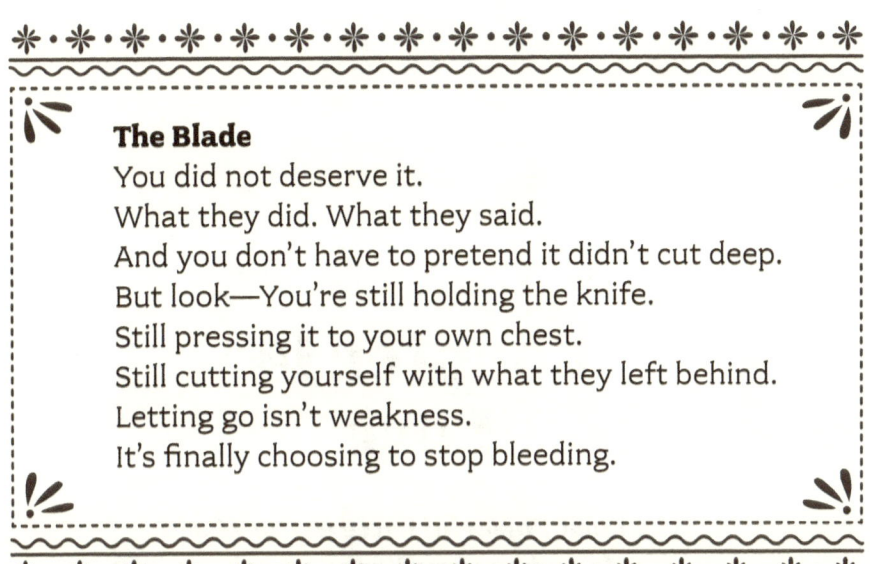

The Blade
You did not deserve it.
What they did. What they said.
And you don't have to pretend it didn't cut deep.
But look—You're still holding the knife.
Still pressing it to your own chest.
Still cutting yourself with what they left behind.
Letting go isn't weakness.
It's finally choosing to stop bleeding.

"Resentment is like setting yourself on fire and hoping the other person dies of smoke inhalation."
— Anne Lamott

"Forgiveness is the fragrance that the violet sheds on the heel that crushed it."
— Mark Twain

Take a moment to think about what you have read.
Let it sink in a bit. Then let the following questions be a guide to where you are, and where you want to be.
Take a moment and really think about them.

Reflections:

• Who do I still carry inside me with anger or pain?

• What would it feel like to release the weight?

• What would forgiveness look like if it were for me, not them?

Chapter 14
Love

The Most Powerful Force in the World.
It's what gives life meaning.

"Three things will last forever—faith, hope,
and love—and the greatest of these is love."
— 1 Corinthians 13:13

We are all going to die.
It's the one guarantee we get.
But while we're still here
while our hearts still beat and our lungs still rise,
we get to choose how we live.

And the only thing that truly makes life worth living...
is **love**.
Not convenience.
Not comfort.
But love that gives, love that heals, love that breathes life
into everything it touches.

Every act of love is an act of rebellion against the grave.
Every time you forgive, stay present, speak kindly, hold
someone's hand, or soften your heart, you push back
against death. **You choose life**.

Love isn't just a feeling.
It's the oxygen of the soul.
It's what keeps us human in a world that's growing numb.
It's how we stay *alive* while we're alive.

You want to live more fully?
Then love more freely.

*"Educating the mind without educating the heart
is no education at all."*
— Aristotle

We often move through life in survival mode, doing what's expected, staying guarded, checking the boxes.

But what if you lived out of love instead of necessity?
What if your life wasn't a reaction, but a gift?
A deliberate outpouring of grace and joy and presence?

Love resurrects you.
It awakens the parts of you the world put to sleep
It reanimates your wonder, your warmth, your humanity.

Because when you live from love, you're not just passing time.
You're creating eternity, moment by moment.

"Love is the only force capable of
transforming an enemy into a friend."
— Martin Luther King Jr.

"Hatred stirs up strife, but love covers all offenses."
— Proverbs 10:12

We all die.
But those who love deeply, live loudly.
And their presence echoes long after they're gone.

So love like it's the only thing that matters.
Because in the end... it is.

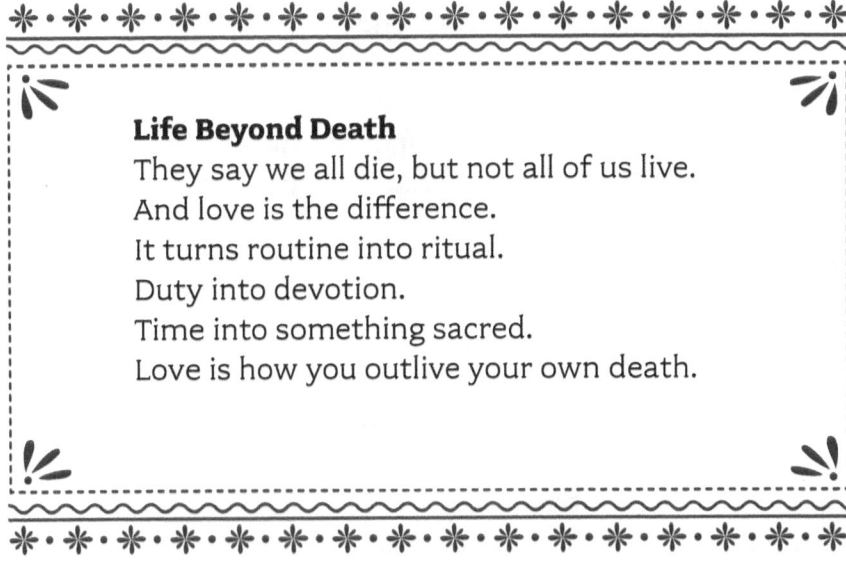

Life Beyond Death
They say we all die, but not all of us live.
And love is the difference.
It turns routine into ritual.
Duty into devotion.
Time into something sacred.
Love is how you outlive your own death.

Love is the only sane and satisfactory answer
to the problem of human existence."
— Erich Fromm

"When the power of love overcomes the love
of power, the world will know peace."
—Jimi Hendrix

Take a moment to think about what you have read.
Let it sink in a bit. Then let the following questions be a
guide to where you are, and where you want to be.
Take a moment and really think about them.

Reflections:

• Who do I love fiercely—and do they know it?

• Where in my life do I need to love more boldly or more honestly?

• Have I forgotten to love myself in the process of loving others?

• When death comes, what do you want to be remembered for?

We were born knowing it would end.

This life is fleeting and fragile, it moves quickly toward its closing chapter. And yet, somewhere between birth and the grave, we're given a chance to make it mean something.

Death is the great equalizer.
But love...
Love is the great distinguisher.

It's what separates the ones who live from the ones who merely survive.
It's the echo that outlasts our bodies.
It's the fingerprint we leave on souls.
And it's the one thing we carry with us when everything else is left behind.

Some say the opposite of death is life.
But maybe, **it's love**.
Because love brings life to what was lifeless.
It revives what we let die inside.
It makes even suffering sacred.
Love isn't weakness. It isn't naive.

"Whoever does not love does not know God,
because God is love."
— 1 John 4:8

It's the most divine thing we are capable of.
And when we act from love, real love, we are touching
something eternal.

So let this be your reminder:
You will die.
But how you love, now, here, in this breath —
is how you live forever.

Live boldly.
Love fully.
Make memories.
Tell stories.

And leave this world softer than you found it.

Chapter 15
The Divine Mystery of Life and Death

We are stardust with a soul, breath held between two eternities.

"What you are is God's gift to you.
What you become is your gift to God."
— Hans Urs von Balthasar

No one makes it out alive.
That's the rule.

But we spend our days pretending otherwise.
Building empires of distraction.
Chasing youth. Avoiding silence.
Treating death like a distant rumor instead of the only
guarantee.

And yet,
it is death that gives life its urgency.
It is mystery that gives life its meaning.

We are born into this world naked, screaming, gasping for air.
And we leave it in silence.
One breath—then none.

In between?
A flash of light.
A blink.
A story made of moments, choices, love, loss, struggle,
stillness and then it's all over.

"You were born with wings.
Why prefer to crawl through life?"
— Rumi

"To the well-organized mind, death is but
the next great adventure."
— J.K. Rowling

We fear death because we don't understand it.
But what if it's not the end?
What if it's the beginning again?
The mystics called it return.
The Stoics called it nature.
The prophets called it home.

Everything that lives must end.
And everything that ends returns to something greater.
Dust to dust.
Spirit to spirit.
Story to eternity.

Stoic Wisdom:
"You could leave life right now.
Let that determine what you do, say, and think."
— Marcus Aurelius

We are not meant to live forever.
But we are meant to live fully.

The divine mystery is not only in death,
but in the fact that we get to live at all.

We are stardust given breath.
Atoms arranged with intention.
Each heartbeat a borrowed miracle.

What will you do with it?

"As a well-spent day brings happy sleep,
so a life well-used brings happy death."
— Leonardo da Vinci

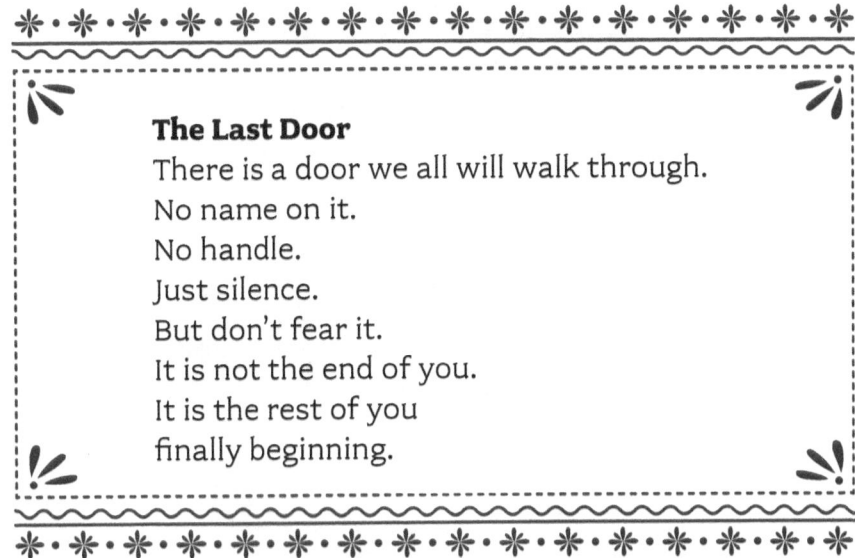

The Last Door
There is a door we all will walk through.
No name on it.
No handle.
Just silence.
But don't fear it.
It is not the end of you.
It is the rest of you
finally beginning.

"Death is not extinguishing the light; it is only putting out the lamp because the dawn has come.
— Rabindranath Tagore

"Live your life so that the fear of death can never enter your heart."
— Tecumseh

Take a moment to think about what you have read. Let it sink in a bit. Then let the following questions be a guide to where you are, and where you want to be. *Take a moment and really think about them.*

Reflections:

• What would change if I lived with the awareness that my time is limited?

• What mystery have I been avoiding out of fear?

• Am I living like my life is sacred?

You don't need all the answers.
You don't need to solve the mystery.
You just need to live the question well

Live.
Love.
Let go.

And when the time comes, walk through the door with your head high and your soul wide open.

To live in hearts we leave behind is not to die"
— Thomas Campbell

"The fear of death follows from the fear of life.
A man who lives fully is prepared to die at any time."
— Mark Twain

"Life should not be a journey to the grave with the intention of arriving safely in a pretty and well preserved body, but rather to skid in broadside in a cloud of smoke, thoroughly used up, totally worn out, and loudly proclaiming "Wow! What a Ride!"
— Hunter S. Thompson

"Everyone dies,
not everyone really lives."

We're here for the ones who do.

— The Skullys

Final Thoughts

A quiet reminder before you go.

You made it to the end.
But maybe this isn't the end at all.
Maybe it's just the beginning, of the version of you that stops waiting,
stops hiding,
and starts living with your soul wide open.

I don't know what you're carrying.
What you've lost.
What you're still trying to forgive.

But I know this much:
You're still here.
Which means the story isn't over.

Whatever this book stirred in you, whether it cracked something open or stitched something closed, I hope it gave you more than just words.
I hope it gave you permission.
Permission to be real.
To begin again.
To feel it all.
To live awake.

The truth is, you never needed this book.
You just needed a moment of stillness.
A mirror.
A match.
A reminder.
That your time here is short.
That your voice matters.
That your wounds are holy.
That being gentle is not the same as being weak.
And that you are allowed to want more.

So here it is, your permission slip:
Go live your life.
Not the half-version.
Not the safe one.
The full one, the raw one, the one burning with passion.

William Shakespeare famously wrote "We are born to die"
Well I say "We are born to live"

And when the doubt creeps in and the world tries to put
you back to sleep, remember:

You weren't put on this earth to struggle through life.
There are no extra people—no one was born by accident.
Your life has a purpose and meaning.
You were not born to die.
You were born to live.

With all my heart,

Fernando Acevedo
The Skullys

Author's Note
From Fernando Acevedo

If you made it here, thank you!
Not just for reading, but for walking beside me through this
manifesto of the soul.

I didn't write this to impress anyone.
I wrote because I needed to hear something real.
I wrote it to tell the truth.

The truth that life is ugly yet beautiful, good and bad, messy,
complicated and most of all it's sacred.
That we all suffer,
we all search,
and we all get only *a small flicker of time* to make it count.

To be honest, this book didn't start as a book.
It started as a personal search.
I've struggled with finding meaning.
I've questioned everything, my place in the world,
my purpose, what any of this means.
And the more I learned, the more lost I sometimes felt.

So I started writing.
Not because I had the answers, but because I was desperate to hear something true.
And I thought, maybe...
if I could help someone else find their way, I might find mine too.

Funny thing is, what I wrote for others turned out to be exactly what I needed to hear.

This book helped me.
It healed something in me.
And if it stirred something in you, then we're not alone in this.

We are not here to drift through life.
We are here to live it fully, wildly, consciously.
To create meaning in the face of chaos.
To choose life while death waits for us.
To choose love even when it hurts.
To stay present again and again, even when it would be easier to stay numb.

You don't have to have it all figured out.
You just have to stay real, stay present, and keep moving forward.

If these words stirred something in you... keep going.

Live Boldly, Love Fully, Make Memories and Tell Stories!

Leave something behind that lives in people's hearts.

With love,
Fernando Acevedo

www.ingramcontent.com/pod-product-compliance
Lightning Source LLC
Chambersburg PA
CBHW031249120626
46545CB00007B/2726